To Jan

thanks for
your help!

CWP

Also by Steve Kowit

Climbing the Walls
Cutting Our Losses
Heart in Utter Confusion
Lurid Confessions
Passionate Journey
Pranks
Mysteries of the Body
For My Birthday
Epic Journeys, Unbelievable Escapes
The Dumbbell Nebula
Steve Kowit: Greatest Hits 1978–2003

On Writing:
In the Palm of Your Hand: The Poet's Portable Workshop

Anthologies:
The Maverick Poets (edited)

Translation:
Incitement to Nixonicide and Praise for the Chilean Revolution, Pablo Neruda

THE GODS OF RAPTURE
Poems in the Erotic Mood

Steve Kowit

**SAN DIEGO
CITY WORKS
PRESS**

THE GODS OF RAPTURE

ISBN 0-9765801-3-6

Library of Congress Control Number: 2006920987

San Diego City Works Press is a nonprofit press, funded by local writers and friends of the arts, committed to the publication of fiction, poetry, creative nonfiction, and art by members of the San Diego City College community and the community at large. For more about San Diego City Works Press, please visit our website at www.cityworkspress.org. The San Diego Writers Collective is extremely indebted to the American Federation of Teachers, Local 1931, without whose generous contribution, this book would not be possible.

Cover Design: Perry Vasquez
Front cover photograph of Kajuraho sculpture: Jaroslav Bech
Back cover art: Peter F. Van Peenen
Production Editor: Will Dalrymple

Published in the United States by San Diego City Works Press, California

Printed in the United States of America

Mary—under the guise of these ancient tales...

Contents

Art

A Prefatory Note

Love is a perennial theme. No subject has been sung with such constancy by so many cultures. Among the greatest of such songs is the amatory poetry of India, a poetry composed in what Sanskrit prosodists call *srngararasa*, the erotic mood. With tenderness, passion and grace, those poets transmuted into song almost every aspect of human love, from the rapture of the first adolescent embrace to the grief of age and irrevocable loss.

From English-language translations of that material I have taken situations that charmed or moved me and shaped them to my own taste. Often an idea or a single line or a vivid image in one or another English-language translation would send me to my notebook or keyboard. So the poems in this collection, most of which bear little or no resemblance to the verses from which they emerged, are not translations—nor are they adaptations. Except for the dedicatory verse that begins this sequence (*after Utpalaraja*), which is an explicit adaptation based on Daniel H. H. Ingalls' literal version, the poems in this volume are simply new poems based on ancient themes.

In several cases there was no particular poem at all that inspired mine—just a general tone or gesture or phrase that came from that ancient verse. Where there were several poems or no specific poem that triggered my own, I have simply tagged the piece *after the Sanskrit* or *after the Tamil*.

My great thanks go to Mark Melnicove, who published *Heart in Utter Confusion*, a handful of these poems, in a 1984 chapbook illustrated by Richard Denner, several of whose lovely linocuts appear on the pages of this book as well. My thanks also to Michael Helm, who published *Passionate Journey* in 1985, a larger collection of them, illustrated by Arthur Okamura. My great thanks go to Jim Miller

xii

and the City Works Collective for permitting this entire sequence of poems—written over the course of many years—to finally see the light of print. My thanks also to Perry Vasquez who designed the cover (and contributed several graphics) and to Will Dalrymple, layout and production editor for City Works Press. I am extremely grateful to the artists whose works grace these pages: I am delighted to have their work accompany my own. Any public thanks I could offer my beloved wife Mary, who served this project as copy editor (and who contributed two of the graphics), would understate her steadfast inspiration, assistance and loving support.

A brief note on those ancient poets of India appears at the end of the book along with a list of the translations of which I made use. Almost without exception those translations are charming and appealing works and I recommend them with enthusiasm. I know of nothing quite like this tradition of love poetry in our own literature or in the literature of any other culture.

The poems themselves need little exegesis. The skillful archer of the dedicatory verse is not Cupid but Kama, Hindu God of Love. Jayadeva, Vidyāpati and the Bengali poets often took for their subject the passionate encounter between the youthful Krishna and the beautiful cowherd Radha. Although I have masked the identity of those protagonists and the divine nature of that erotic tale, it is my hope that now and again in these poems some of the irresistible music of Lord Krishna's flute might still be heard.

—Steve Kowit

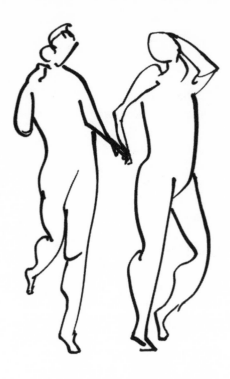

Behold the archer's skill
that leaves the body whole
but breaks the heart.

after Utpalaraja

4

What chord did she pluck in my soul
that girl with the golden necklace
& ivory breasts
whose body ignited the river:
she who rose like the moon
from her bathing &
brushed back the ebony hair
that fell to her waist
& walked off
into the twilight dark—
O my soul,
what chord did she pluck
that I am still trembling?

after Chandidās

That little girl across the road
was spinning cartwheels
only yesterday it seems
& yet today I hardly recognized her
when she passed,
she'd grown so much.
Grown? No, she was transfigured!
What a swiveling of hips,
what lush young breasts!
I think, perhaps, she did not
recognize me either,
for instead of the familiar,
playful greeting I anticipated
she just glanced at me an instant,
blushed, & looked away.

                    after Kālidāsa

What need
for you to stretch
your arms
behind your throat
& bind your braid
so that your back
arches
& your weight
falls gracefully
to one hip
& buttock
as your breasts rise?
Child,
it is superfluous—
those glances
of your dark eyes
are enough.

after Viryamitra

When the water lily opens
in the fresh spring
it has not her charm.
Nor has the white moonlight
spilling over the hills.
When she moves
she sways
like a field of grain
in a summer breeze
but with more grace.
Even the peacock
is not as lovely as she.

after the Tamil

You
who have been held
to her breasts
& cradled
against her thighs
& upon whom she plays
with such passion
& skill
are indeed to be envied
O lute
of that marvelous girl
with the dark eyes.
I too,
God knows,
would make rapturous
music.

after Vācaspati

Someone is playing a flute
on the banks of the swollen Yamuna.
On the pastureland of Gokula,
that country of cowherds,
someone is playing a flute
that awakens such longing
a woman is helpless before it.
Trembling & golden
it floats thru the afternoon
engulfing its victim in raptures
of amorousness & desire
—the housework untouched,
the heart in utter confusion.

after Chandidās

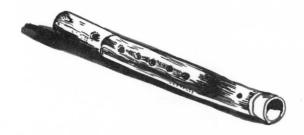

Others saw him too
as he stood at the edge
of the ripening field
asking for work.
                He
who held a canvas satchel
over his shoulder came,
he said, from the land
where the summer west wind
makes flute music
out of the little holes
that the bees bore
in the swaying bamboo,
& the cold water falling
over the rocks
is the music of drums,
& monkeys shriek
when a peacock
dances about
on one of the hills
like a young woman.
                Friend,
is it possible
I am the only one of all
those who saw him that day
who tosses about in bed,
night after night,
with a grief
nothing has caused,
& arms clutching the darkness?

after the Tamil

I bent my head
to stop my eyes
from stealing glances
but they rose again
to drink that face,
& when I lowered them
again they rose.
& so I closed my
eyes & suddenly
I was floating,
borne away,
miraculously
soaring—
O something
in that instant
opened
in my body
like a spray of light,
a lifting
of golden plumage,
an exaltation of wings.

after Vidyāpati

Since first I heard his name
it has overcome my heart
& thrown my life into confusion—
I cannot get enough.
I whisper it all day
& half the night.
It is intoxicating.
I have grown so drunk upon it
I have lost all semblance of control
& am responsible for nothing
that I do—especially today,
for my addiction took a fatal turn
when I discovered where he lives
& when he is likely to be home,
& how can an innocent girl
defend herself against that?
May heaven protect me!
If his name alone is heady enough
to drive me insane,
god knows what will happen tonight
when I taste his lips!

after Dwija Chandidās

The party began quietly
with small groups strolling
about the garden & chatting.
But the full moon
of the first night of summer
rose overhead
like a ripe orange
& the music grew hot
& the wine flowed
& now these young women
are no longer shy
but have kicked off their shoes
& thrown back their hair
& are dancing out on the lawn
by the mossy pond
in the throbbing & moonlit dark—
tongues of grass
under their naked feet
& the night air touched with magnolia.

after Vidyāpati

Where the swollen Monongahela
washes the Alleghenies,
wind perfumes the air with fine pollen
& butterflies flicker among the vines
& birds
abandoning all modesty
sing of paradise
in the cool branches.
Here young girls
whirl about on the hillside,
their summer dresses
billowing out
like colorful petals.
Soon, young men will join them
& they will shriek with delight
& chase each other & dance
& couple
by couple vanish
into the swaying field
where honeybees feast
on the bells
of delicate flowers.

after the Sanskrit

Do not speak to me of that irresistible flute
at whose plaintive & passionate note
the devoted housewife
slips from her couch,
drawn like a thirsty doe to the stream,
& the mendicant sage
who dreamed he'd forsaken
the world of illusory forms
strays from the True Path.
Seduced by that haunting air,
even the aged & infirm
make fools of themselves.
Friend, if even the tiniest creatures
dance rapturously
when they hear that promiscuous flute,
what chance does an innocent
girl such as I—already
more than half mad with desire—
have to resist?

after Chandidās

Though she enjoys
slipping her lips
to my mouth
when no one is looking
& doesn't object
to my hand
fondling her breast,
she is still like a child
who loves to ride
around in a toy cart
& gallop about on a horse
whose tail
is a piece of rope
nailed to a broom
handle, & has not yet
got the idea
of the pleasure
of mounting something
faster moving than that
& life-sized.

after Tumpicērkiran

Because they are both innocent & young,
instead of consummation's brazen
flames, their hearts burn rather
with the hesitant, erratic sparks
of bashfulness & longing.
First passion overcomes them & then fright:
whatever conflagration
will consume their flesh
some future moon-intoxicated night,
this night, all night, however seared
by mutual desire, they do & do not dare.

after Lakṣmīdhara

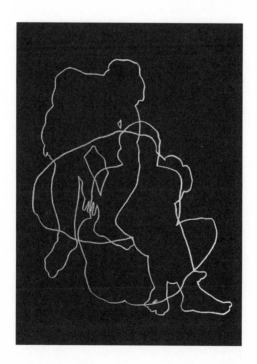

Catching an unexpected peek
of the polished slope
of her lovely breasts
the young man
seems as astonished
as if he had suddenly
discovered himself
on a sheer ledge
high in the Himalayas
from which,
he can see at once,
he will never escape.

after Pānini

A half-grown girl went to bathe
& ate a green mango
washed up on the shore.
How could she know
it was from the king's
sacred tree?
                        Yet
for that crime
he refused eighty-one bull elephants
& a doll
wrought of the girl's
weight in gold,
&
        (may that tyrant
        writhe in eternal flames)
had her killed.
                        May my mother also
go straight to Hell
for guarding too well
the fruit of her womb:
since that young boarder
rented the room next to mine,
she will not leave my side,
& at night, lies awake
like a fortress
                about to be stormed.

after Paraṇar

After lessons & devotions,
when her classmates
gather at the garden bench
to giggle over secret crushes
& infatuations,
she will feign an interest
just sufficient so that
no one notes
her awkward silence,
or the flush
about her cheeks,
& pallor at her lips.
How fearful she has grown
that one of them
might guess
what even she
can hardly fathom—she,
a priestess of forbidden
bliss, those fearful
but exquisite moonlit rites
consecrated
to the gods of rapture.

after Narasiṃha

Mother hums in the kitchen.
Father tosses a handful
of branches
onto the hearth,
kindles the fire,
& settles back
into his chair.
Baby brother, purring,
spins a wheel of his toy cart.
But daughter?
Daughter
is nowhere about.
From the boathouse trees
at the edge of the lake,
with a sudden clapping
of wings,
birds
fly into the moon.

      after the Sanskrit

If she denies it she is lying—
there were witnesses:
two purple gallinules
among the spatterdock;
a heron,
standing motionless
on one long
reed-like leg;
& silver minnows
leaping
in the moon-drenched waters.

after Kapilar

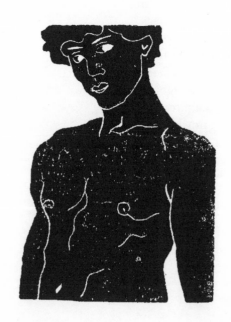

I was so drunk
on the sweet wine
of her mouth
that my teeth
left marks
on her breasts
& drew blood.
With her eyes
half closed
& her tongue
licking
the soft bulb
of her upper
lip, she
put her finger
there
& touched it
very slowly
& sucked
her breath in.

after Bilhaṇa

Those purple tokens on
her breasts
& thighs
are neither blemishes
nor in the least
unsightly.
She takes them, rather,
as delicious gifts,
seals that mark her
as a votary,
beloved
of The Lord
Who Draws the Bow.

after Dakṣa

There was no hint he might come.
There was no reason
to expect him.
Yet throughout the night
while the others slept
I could hear
the sapphire-
blue flowers
from that tree
at the end of the garden
being torn
by the wind
& falling.

after Kollan Arici

Fearing that she'll give herself away,
she dares not look at him,
but to the others offers up
opinions about matters
she knows nothing of,
distractedly begins to stroke
her niece's silken hair,
then, for no reason, scolds the child,
draws the poor thing to her,
hugs her fiercely,
kisses her a dozen times
&, all but weeping, tells her what a
precious dear sweet little thing she is.

after Amaru

Because she has been running thru a summer downpour
& arrives at the young man's apartment all
disheveled, breathless, rain-
drops dripping from her hair, her
sandals drenched, her sheer
blue sundress wringing wet
& clinging to her,
is it any wonder
after only one embrace,
solicitous of his beloved's welfare,
the young man quickly helps her out of her wet things?

after Yogésvara

Her mouth says no but her limbs are aflame.
No—& she offers her throat to his lips.
No…no…& is thus disrobed.
demurring,
& is rocked in his arms
whispering No…
no…
ever so softly,
over & over.

after Abhinanda

Mother, do not expect me till late.
Though I like the boy's company
his car is an old hunk of tin
with a penchant for puttering out
a hundred miles from nowhere.
By the time we get the thing
rolling again,
my dress will be ravaged,
my hair & makeup a mess,
& my neck & throat painfully bruised.
No doubt, by the time we return
the night will be all but spent.
Mother, I beg you: do not wait up!

after the Sanskrit

After thrashing
in a thousand
motions
taught by love,
she snuggles
in the pillow
of his arms,
& breathing
peacefully
at last
—a hint
of satisfaction
at her lips—
falls fast asleep.

after Pradyumna

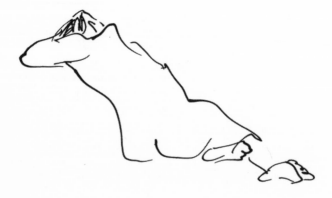

Awakening as fresh young sprigs of light
open in the east, & seeing
that the master of her revels
is already dressed,
she springs out of her bed,
sniffs his hair & throat,
& cautions
that he dare not hazard home
with her enticing scent
so evident upon him.
No! he dare not even step
into the street
till she has bathed him thoroughly
—to which altogether sensible
suggestion he most readily assents.

after Murāri

In the morning
my love comes to me
& we play on a couch
by the window
thru which flows
the delicious scent
of lilac & alyssum,
& now & then
I play for her
upon my silver flute
that song she so loves.
An hour past midday
she showers,
shedding the honeyed
perfumes of love,
& redoes her hair,
& powders,
& wriggles back
into her skirt,
& is home
before she has even
been missed.
All evening,
barefoot,
she dances
about that house,
her face lit
with that little song
that nobody hears,
or hearing,
thinks anything of.

after Kapilar

In the morning,
holding her mirror,
the young woman
touches
her tender
lip
with her finger
& then with the tip
of her tongue
licks it
& smiles
& admires her eyes.

after the Sanskrit

If God created me
why then
did he create a boy
of such athletic build?
Or having made us both,
why lips?
Or if he must have lips,
why then did he call forth the moon,
or spring,
or night,
or if he was compelled
to make these too,
why then did he create
soft reeds
along the river
in the moonlight—
surely the undoing of us all.

after Vīryamitra

As I stepped out of my skirt
all my chagrin
fell away.
He was so lovely
& I
quenching my thirst
with his body
was wholly delighted.
Only now
do I color with shame
recalling
how stupid I was
to be taken in by his lies.

after Vidyāpati

Daughter, what you mistook for torrential love
was a brief squall.
His tempestuousness?
…A passing wind lifting your skirt.

after Śrī Harṣa-Deva

It was brutal. A country boy
without an iota of skill
in the art of lovemaking,
he scratched up my back,
manhandled my breasts,
bit on my throat,
& when he finally entered,
his boyish strength
was too much for me.
He was immense—
savage—
insatiable!
I pleaded & cried out,
but in vain.
I swear,
had the vow
not been sealed with a kiss
I would never meet him
again tonight
as I promised I would.
But it was,
& I cannot go back on my word—
it is out of the question.
I would run over thorns
with my bare feet
to be there on time—
for with me,
as you well know,
honor comes first!

after Vidyāpati

Daughter, when you frisk with the cat
take more care. See
that small discoloration
by your throat…
            & there,
those scratches on your breasts
& back?
Learn to play less passionately, dear.
—Mama, whatever are you driving at?
The roses that I gathered for the house
were full of thorns.

                        after Sonnoka

Mother, it's the freezing wind
that's brought such color to my cheeks
& disarrayed my hair
& made my lips so tender.
Why this woolen scarf
has even bruised my throat.
See—look here—
No, mother,
I have not met anyone!

after Dharmadāsa

One hand undid the knot
of her robe; the other
lifted the golden necklace
caressing her breasts.

after Bilhaṇa

When he pressed his lips to my mouth
the knot fell open of itself.
When he pressed them to my throat
the dress slipped to my feet.
So much I know—but
when his lips touched my breast
everything, I swear,
down to his very name,
became so much confused
that I am still,
dear friends,
unable to recount
(as much as I would care to)
what delights
were next bestowed upon me
& by whom.

after Vikaṭanitambā

I nearly choked with laughter
when the doctor
that my mother sent me to
tried psychogarbilitic
doubletalk
to cure
these fits of constant sighing
                              (gift
of that lanky, dark-
haired boy with amber eyes).
More exercise! he ordered.
More fresh air!
& lots of rest! You'll have
to spend more time in bed!
Spend more time in bed?
I covered up
my nervous giggles
with a fit
of coughing—almost
choked—while promising
him faithfully I would.

after Llango Adigal

The moment that my name is mentioned
she is buried in her purse
or finds a hangnail that needs prompt attention
or a thread that's suddenly come unraveled
in her sleeve.
If someone laughs
she colors—certain
that the worst has happened
& the game is up
& everybody knows.

after Śrī Harṣa-Deva

I'd rather be nipped by a rabid fox
than be stung by your eyes.
The antivenin for rabies
is painful indeed.
But for the heart driven mad
there is no cure whatsoever.

After Bhartṛhari

Beloved, could they be whetstones
—those dark spots
on the moon—
to sharpen the arrows of passion
grown blunt
from the breaking of too many hearts?

after Ganapati

Joyful is he who tastes his bride's red mouth
in a thatched pavilion screened against the storm
—her moans & quickened breathing
mingling with the drops
that beat all night against the pumpkin vine,
& violent thunderclaps,
& moorhens
crying out against the driving rains.

after Subhānga

Not to have seen her
is to be robbed of Paradise.
To have seen her
is to be robbed of one's heart.

after Prabhākara–Deva

Over the forest
pavilion
a splinter
of lightning
& suddenly
her face
in a nest
of tangled
flowers
& dark hair.
May the song's
mood
echo
the incandescence
of love.

after Jayadeva

Her loveliness defies description.
No god bloated
with dyspeptic righteousness
could have created her.
More likely
she's the daughter of the moon
with its seductive
& incantatory light,
or of some woodland sprite,
or of the warm spring rain—
she who is,
among all the creatures
of this world,
the most ravishing.

after Kālidāsa

Once & for all
put aside
your quibbling
metaphysics
& decide the matter:
shall we attend
upon the sloping
domes
of old cathedrals,
or the curvaceous
buttocks
of voluptuous women?

after Bhartṛhari

Lord knows
I've chanted
& worshipped
& fasted
& meditated
& prayed
my whole life.
Still,
the sight
of her youthful
body
the moment
my fingers
undo
the clasp
of her dress
is as close
as I think
I will ever come
to *satori*.

after Śrngāratilaka

When no one looks she'll catch
his eye & blow a kiss
at him across the room,
or with her index finger
slowly stroke her thigh,
or slide her tongue salaciously
along her upper lip—
gestures that,
if she were caught,
might well unleash a storm
that would undo them both.
At once, for his part,
flustered & enflamed, he
looks away & coughs
that nervous cough.
How many times
he's scolded her
to be more circumspect!
& yet, that she
is irrepressibly provocative
& mischievous
& bold,
renders, he well understands,
their stolen nights together
rapturous
beyond his most
extravagant, forbidden dreams.

after Parameśvara

Hooked in by heaving sighs
& pouting lips
& trembling breasts,
we poor bedeviled fish
first lose our heads
& then,
upon the glowing coals
of our own lust,
are sizzled crisp.

after Bhartṛhari

In the madness
of the white light
of the moon,
near high reeds
where croaking frogs,
beating like drums,
frightened
a small bird
from the field,
I trembled,
& he swore
he would not leave me.

after the Tamil

I've been betrayed!
I see it in their eyes!
Among his snickering friends
my name is now an object
of amusement.
Oh, I am mortified.
How could he be so cruel?
I offered him my love.
Instead, he took my virtue
& my reputation.

after Venputi

Fool—
The touch
of her lips
is the inescapable
trap!
In the lotus's
passionate
petals
closing about it,
the bee
hovers,
bewitched.

after Bhartṛhari

Once, had I offered
you the green
fruit of the margosa,
how delectable
it would have seemed
—how ripe & sweet.
But now,
were I to offer you
the freshest
morning water
of the mountain stream,
how bitter you
would claim it tastes.
Beloved,
nothing I can ever
offer you again
will gladden you
or slake your thirst.

after the Tamil

He's left!
With his damn flute!
If you come across any reeds
on one of your walks,
rip them out of the ground,
tear them up by the roots,
fling them into the sea!

after Chandidās

Here I've suffered unspeakable
anguish & this jerkwater town
scratches its fat behind
in its sleep
as if nothing were wrong.
Not a living soul
takes note of my grief.
Nobody cares
if I die of a shattered heart.
Do I have to beat them
over the head with a stick,
wring their dumb necks,
burn the place to the ground
before they have the slightest
inkling that the boy
who made me
all those splendid promises
is gone?

after the Sanskrit

Now when the fragrant breeze
in the mountain
lifts back the wild vines
& touches the clover,
& he is off roaming the country,
dancing with young women,
the pointed leaves of the eucalyptus
tear at my heart.

after Jayadeva

Though he for whom
I cannot help but wait
has wandered half the world
& I already be forgotten,
I shall not forget.
O violent waves,
though you erase
with every onslaught
on the beach
our bodies' traces
tangled in the strand,
can you erase my heart?
O sacred sea,
are you, too, unable
to forget
your ancient lover—
you who wail all night?

after Llango Adigal

Till you rise again
over the rim
of the sea,
lend me,
I beg you,
O vanishing sun,
a few small rays,
that I may search for him.

after the Tamil

The city is sheer delight
with its markets
& highways
& elegant restaurants
& theaters
& parks
& the women—
the women
every bit as fetching
as everyone said
they would be.
& the climate perfect—
absolutely ideal!
Only sometimes,
at night,
walking along the beach
over the twisted roots
of the mangroves,
the ocean
calls me back
to that girl
with the dark eyes,
& those summer nights
we lay by the raging river
wrapped in each other's arms.
Then I walk back
into a city
of nothing but shrillness
& gaudy illusion.

after Vidyāpati

Sometimes
even the heart
of the man
who seems
perfectly happy
is touched
by the single
thread
of a longing
that cannot be named—
the shred,
perhaps,
of a being
he loved
in another life.

after Kālidāsa

Black crow,
from a golden plate
brimming with fresh ghee
& green meal
will I feed you
& all of your offspring
if you will but caw
the return of him
whose approach
I have heard
everywhere lately—
in the lizard
vanishing
into the brush,
in a sprig of flowers
torn from a tree
by the wind,
in a cupped leaf
spilling its rain.

after the Tamil

Darling, I anticipated your arrival
with the first rains,
but the river is at flood,
the storm is unrelenting,
the sky,
at every crack of thunder,
lights up with a lurid glare,
& still you have not come.
Once again I have sat beside your desk
all evening,
folding & unfolding your letter,
staring out the window at the dark.
Drunk with delight
all the frogs & waterbirds
are shrieking,
& the peacocks dance.
I long for you.
My sorrow is unending.

after Vidyāpati

Dusk,
in the wake
of my grief
over him
to whom
I have given
my heart,
do not
torment me.
Only
the cruelest
of hunters
would
take aim
at a terrified
doe
caught
in a flood
& struggling
for life.

after the Tamil

Darling, you were so far away for so long & I so near death
that I feared we would never see each other again.
But a woman can bear pain
that would shatter a stone
& though each day of that grief felt like a hundred years
I was happy for you, I swear it,
there in that far-off city
with all its diversions & glamour. O my jewel,
holding you now to my breast all that anguish dissolves.
The bees hum in the garden, the birds of the evening
sing to their loves in the gathering dark,
& the moon ascends heaven.

after Chandidās

All night we lay in each other's arms.
The world spilled forth
as if language itself
had come into being
there,
with our love.
We talked about everything…
nothing…
not even dawn stopped us.

after Bhavabhūti

When the moon glows
upon the face of my beloved
such a tide of amorous
desire rises in me
you would think a thousand
moons were pulling
at my heart.
In his arms my life has meaning.
In the soft south breeze
my hair,
which he has loosened,
trembles.
Far away
a nightingale is singing.

after Vidyāpati

Friend, I get no more rest
than I did when he was away
& I spent my nights
tossing in dread
that he would never return.
Now that he is back home
at last
in his own bed,
sleep
is altogether out of the question.

after Vidyāpati

That smudge of mascara by your mouth
& the stench of perfume
clinging to your hair
speak eloquently,
O my beloved. Therefore
do not waste your breath
& put me off with silly lies.
What of it—
you had a night out on the town
with some rouged midinette
with pretty curls
& caught up on all the latest
subtleties of lovemaking.
Do you think I begrudge you that pleasure?
We are not children.
As for the girl, I envy
the loveliness & grace
that must have held you captive
& salute the good luck she had
to have used her night
to such advantage.
But please, O my dearest,
do not, in some attack
of misguided remorse,
blurt out her name—
for having heard it
I will have no recourse
but to find the little
bitch & scratch her eyes out.

after Vidyāpati

Did he who fashioned
your eyes of the lotus,
your hands
of white jasmine,
your body
out of magnolia,
weary of soft things
at last,
& carve your heart
out of stone?

after Bhartṛhari

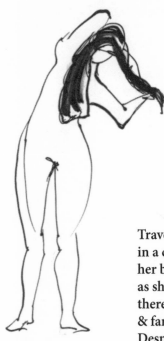

Traveler, she answered
in a charming voice,
her body swaying slightly
as she spoke,
there's nothing in this town but sheep
& farmers who are fast asleep by dusk.
Despite the view,
that grassy field among the hills
that are as sweet & rolling
as a woman's breasts,
there's nothing much to recommend the place.
Still, if you are weary
& would care to spend the night here,
you are welcome to.

after the Sanskrit

When my husband, the Colonel,
is off on maneuvers,
& it's just growing dark,
& the rain pounds on the roof
& steams up the glass,
& the broken-off branches
whip through the street
like a stampede of stallions,
& the wind howls,
I could just die.
I mean, my heart pumps
like mad.
Doubly so
if the guy I'm with
is anywhere cute
& knows what he's doing.

after the Sanskrit

Delighted to be driving
thru a pounding hail
& howling wind storm
in a dark
& unfamiliar
neighborhood
at night,
the adventurous
young housewife
has an address
scribbled on a notepad
on her dashboard,
& a change of clothing
on the seat beside her,
& a husband
who is out of town.

after Jaghanacapalā

May those charming women, whose public
virtue hides a hankering for sin,
whose Sunday faith is to inveigh against
what secretly they most desire,
who for their evening benedictions
wrap themselves in underthings of silk
& lace, bestow upon you
all the sacraments
of that most reverent sisterhood, that sect
of which they are the sacred votaries,
& bless you with their loving grace.

after Vibhoka

Young man, I'm sorry but my husband isn't home.
His mother suffered one of her "attacks"
& telephoned us in the dead of night
& whined on for an hour till he swore
he'd catch the first flight out this morning.
& so off he went.
& I suppose he won't be back till late tomorrow night.
That old fraud can get him to do anything,
whereas he doesn't give a hoot
how lonesome I get
sleeping in this big house all alone.
But enough of that—what is it now
exactly that you're selling?
Look, it's pouring out.
Why don't you come on in
& take that soaking jacket off
& show me what it is you have?
—I mean, who knows, I might be interested.

after Murāri

When he saw those telltale marks
on the flesh of the woman
he worshipped,
he was stunned,
knowing at last
why she had been hiding
herself
those past several nights.
How deeply the teeth
of the one who had bruised
her breasts
in passionate play
tore into his heart.

after Murāri

My husband loves me, I suppose,
as much now
as on those moon-drenched nights
of twenty years ago,
so like tonight
—the very breeze
that blows from the Vindhya hills
still heavy with the scent of jasmine.
I love him also,
yet I yearn
with all my soul
for those reedbeds
along the crooked stream
that shared
our never-ending bouts
of youthful love.

after Śīlābhaṭṭārikā

Dearest, when we were introduced
& became lovers
all my friends approved,
& how delighted they all were
when we exchanged our vows.
& when you bore our children
they couldn't have been more pleased.
But now that we have lived together
more than thirty years
& I have not yet
stopped raving of your gentle grace
& matchless beauty,
my friends just shake their heads,
& roll their eyes, & think me mad.

after the Sanskrit

I practiced at my rage all afternoon:
I'd bite my lip to let him see the fury
under my civility & self-restraint
& offer pleasantries
that cut both ways
& smiles calculated for their cruelty.
So have I whipped myself
into a seething froth
against the risk of being swept away
all misty with forgiveness & devotion.
Not only have I strengthened
my resolve
but tightly bound my skirt
with double knots
that I be obdurate & it well fortified
against the onslaught
of his final argument:
for in such matters nothing is assured.
God knows, if he but touches me I'm lost.

after Dharmakīrti

My hands shake—your letter is unconscionably civil.
Have you then forgotten how it was
that season when our trembling passion blossomed
& our hearts were wedded
less by words than kisses, sighs,
the benedictions of our bodies?
O my beloved, your lips & tongue
that one time could not swear enough devotion
now are given to strange uses:
having once sealed vows, they now seal envelopes
filled with banalities & kind excuses,
& everywhere between the lines
the lethal cruelty of your indifference.

after Ramananda Ray

Beloved,
if you are enraged
torture me
with your tongue,
flay me with your nails,
impale me
with your passionate
touch,
drive me insane
with the heat
of your breasts
& your thighs,
chain me
to your arms,
pummel me
with kisses,
crush me
to your voluptuous heart.

after Jayadeva

If you must go
then I won't stop you,
but stay for an hour
more, or half
an hour or
just a few minutes
longer;
at least
let me look at you,
touch you...
do not run off
before I have even
gotten to know
who you were.
Your voice is so lovely...
let me feel what it's like
to rock in your arms
one last time.
Alive, we are two
small cups of water
running into the sand.
Who knows
if we'll ever
see each other again?

after Amaru

As she stretched to see above the gate
her breasts rose, a breeze
pressed her skirt to her thighs,
the golden band at her waist
trembled.
& always I see her thus, alone in the crowd,
her small hands clutching the rail. Never
have I been held as her eyes held me
at that moment
when I looked back for the last time.

after Rājaśekhara

She stood rooted there—
a young tree
in a great storm,
her steadfast eyes
& heart
climbing the path
he had taken—
the one that leads
past the dry well
& the ruined temple
& the veil-weaver's hut,
then slowly winds
into the endless mountains.

after Kamban

88

In the evening,
weary of the road
& his heart
heavy,
he turns toward home
& lost in contemplation
gazes
at her lovely figure
even now,
though they are separated
by a range of mountains
& a hundred rivers.

after Satyabodha

Cool garland
woven of silver
light. How
much joy they
once took
in the moon
that tonight
sears
like a poisoned
shaft
the trembling
limbs of
the woman
bereft
of her lover.

after Kālidāsa

All day she watched the road
until it was devoured
by the evening.
Evening?
Or was that the goddess
of death,
red & black,
swinging the south wind
like a noose
over that pale face,
that unquiet heart.

after the Tamil

Torment me, sandalwood mountain wind!
Love, festoon me with arrows!
Home of my father
be you never more refuge to me.
O merciless river, Yamuna,
sister of death,
I would drown in the flood of your waters
that this anguish be quenched.

after Jayadeva

For others the scent
of the night-blooming jasmine.
Now that the light
has dwindled & the sun's
rage is spent,
there will come
in the wake of the evening
a darkness
more vast than the sea,
yet of no more use
than a cup of wine
drained to its last dregs,
& a moon that is bitterness.

after the Tamil

In this late summer evening
thick with fragrance,
the birds
have been tormenting me
with their gay songs.
They have no sense
of approaching autumn
or the burst dam of youth.
Their hearts are at flood.
Perhaps in the language of birds
there is no word for tomorrow.
But for me it is otherwise.
In this sweet darkness
their songs
are piercing my heart.

after Vidyāpati

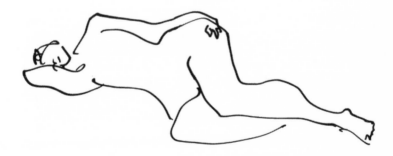

At last,
in a harsh,
almost inaudible whisper
the foreigner
spoke
of the wife
he had left
behind.
          Then
his voice broke
with a moan
so piteous even
now when the story
is told
the quarrels
of lovers cease
& householders
shake
their heads & business-
men consider
postponing
their travels abroad.

after Amaru

Does that girl who used to gather hibiscus
at dusk, by the river,
recall our nights of abandoned love
in the reeds
& know that my heart is still hers,
or do only the screaming parrots remember?

after Kapilar

Pathetic & ephemeral the coupling of lovers.
A moment at best
& even that an illusion.
Bound to the wheel of desire
                              —O bitter
& miserable fate!
& yet,
though I meditate on this truth
for a thousand years
it will not erase the sound of her voice
in the summer night
or the taste of her lips.

                              after Dharmakīrti

How easy to lose one's way
in the cascade of a woman's hair.
& swimmers stronger by far
than yourself
have been swept away
by a passionate glance.
Beware torrential floods,
blistering heat,
violent & unpredictable storms,
the treacherous plunge
from slippery thighs
& precipitous breasts,
for many who enter
the vale of desire never return.
Traveler, you are warned:
proceed at your own risk!

after Rājaśekhara

Seeker—even those who scorn
the illusion of the senses
& spurn the delusive
snare of the flesh,
whose minds are fixed
on *Samadhi,* Liberation,
& their own breath,
breathe heavily
among voluptuous women.

after Bhartṛhari

Even now
I recall
how shyly
she tried
to disentangle
herself
from my arms,
raising the rose
I had brought
to her small face.
—O how lovely
the scent!
she cried out,
hoping, thereby,
to shield
her heart
from that flame
kindled
a moment before
at our lips.

after Bilhaṇa

Even now
I crush in my arms
like a madman
that girl with
vermilion lips
& lush breasts.
I ravish her mouth
like a parched root
drinking the rain.

after Bilhaṇa

Even now I
remember holding
on tight for
that wild
ride her
legs kicking
head thrown
back in a
rapture of
tumbled hair,
luster of moon
lighting
her shivering
body,
lush breasts
heaving with sighs.

after Bilhaṇa

Even now
though they sever
my soul
from my body
I brood
on her fragile
forbidden
beauty,
that wild pheasant
whose dance
scattered
the pollen
of delicate
flowers.
May she
whom I will not
meet again
in this world
& for whose
love I am
borne to my grave
be my fate
in the next life
as well.

after Bilhaṇa

Let the flame of my passion
glow in the eyes of my beloved.
Let it illuminate our path.
Let the liquid
of which our bodies are composed
be at once the river refreshing us
& the well
at which we quench our thirst.
Let our spirits be the air
we breathe
& thru which we move
till we are no longer ourselves,
& I lie by my beloved's side
in the earth.
Let our dusts be one.

after Govindadāsa

Now I am nothing
but the shadow
of the girl I was.
How forthrightly
they look at me
who one day
would have passed
with furtive glances.

after Śatānanda

Cosmetics do no good:
not shadow, rouge, mascara, lipstick—
nothing helps.
However artfully I comb my hair,
embellishing my throat & wrists with jewels,
it is no use—there is
no semblance of the beautiful young girl
I was
& long for still.
My loveliness is past.
& no one could be more aware than I am
that coquettishness at this age
only renders me ridiculous.
I know it. Nonetheless,
I primp myself before the glass
like an infatuated schoolgirl
fussing over every detail,
practicing whatever subtlety
may please him.
I cannot help myself.
The God of Passion has his will of me
& I am tossed about
between humiliation & desire,
rectitude & lust,
disintegration & renewal,
ruin & salvation.

after Vidyāpati

As a young woman she had been courted
by boys who seemed foolish
& coarse. Then a young man
who enflamed her passions seduced
& betrayed her. Another
treated her poorly. & one disappointment
led to the next till she gave
up on the whole sorry business.
Disillusioned & chastened, she taught
school in that village for thirty-six years.
She had a few devoted friends & a sister
whose four children she dearly loved
& whom she would shower with gifts.
& thus did she age, there,
alone, where others mated & wed
& gave birth. Sometimes,
on beautiful summer days,
she would stroll through the fields
to a pond in the woods not far
from the house where she had lived
as a child, & the small plot of land
where her parents were buried,
& there she would sit at the water's edge
watching the dragonflies scurry about,
& the bright, silvery fish just
under the surface dart here & there,
like nervous citizens plagued by things
they were certain had to get done.
Then she would smile
& relish her life & give thanks
for this beautiful & mysterious world.

after the Tamil

It was a warm night. A bright gibbous moon
shone through the bedroom window
of the small house
they had recently purchased
for the sake of the family
they were planning to start.
The next morning he would leave for the front.
They lay, after love, talking softly
of how wonderful, when he returned,
everything was going to be.
Then they grew silent & he touched his index
finger slowly to the bridge of her nose,
traced the lines of her lips,
& brushed with its tip, ever so softly,
the lids of her eyes.
A peacock cried out from a neighbor's yard.
Then he whispered her name
& thanked her—
though for what he did not say,
nor did she ask.
How well & often lying there
in that very bed, by herself,
those many years since that night,
she remembered
that bright gibbous moon, the peacock's cry
in the dark, the touch
of his finger tracing her face, his voice
thanking her, quietly, without explanation.

after the Tamil

Unable to bear
the sight
of her last
staggering steps
& raising
his great head,
the mate
of the wounded elephant
bellows at heaven
again & again
shaking the forest,
the whole world
with his grief.

after the Tamil

The terrible cry he let out
when he heard of her death
shattered the mountain
& pierced his own life
& he fell unconscious.
Child,
even now
when the deer remember,
the grass falls out of their mouths.

after Kṣemendra

Summer days, decades
ago, I would lie
by your side in
the shade of the willow
tree that was here
on the riverbank. One
day I would have
carved our names
on its bark
with a small knife
had you not said
no, do not harm it.
That day we swore
to love each other forever.
Uprooted,
that tree has been gone
many years. Now
you too are no more.
Today I stroll on the bank
by the thrashing waters
here where it stood
recalling your voice
& the beauty
& gentle grace
of your spirit—this river
that rushes
headlong into the sea....

after the Sanskrit

Bow to Kama
God of Love
who has overpowered
Siva,
Brahma,
Vishnu,
& everybody else.

after Bhartṛhari

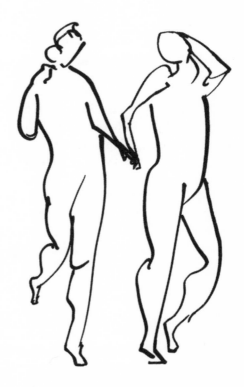

Darling, these are the songs
of your long hair,
your soft voice,
& dark eyes,
that I have always
wanted to write.
Now I have done so
under the guise
of these ancient tales
of the love of Radha
& Krishna:
that girl who tended
the gentle beasts
of the Vrindavan fields
where the sacred
Yamuna flows,
& the Lord of the Flute.

after the Sanskrit

Sources

The Poets

Llango Adigal, Kapilar, Kollan Arici, Kṣemendra, Paraṇar and Tum-picērkīran were Tamil poets who lived in the first few centuries of the current era. Llango Adigal wrote the great Tamil epic "Silappadhiga-ram" around the year 180. Kapilar and Paraṇar are considered to be two of the greatest poets of their age. Kamban, considered the greatest of medieval Tamil poets, was born in the 9th century.

Chandidās, Dwija Chandidās, Ramananda Ray and Vidyāpati were medieval Bengali poets: Vidyāpati wrote in Maithili, the others in the Bengali language. All other poets cited wrote in Sanskrit. With a few exceptions—notably Kālidāsa, the greatest of classical Sanskrit poets, who lived in the 4th or 5th century, and Bhartṛhari, who is thought to have lived around 400—their work was composed between the 8th and 12th centuries.

The Texts

The following books are the sources of these poems. They are all highly recommended.

Bhattacharya, Deben. *Love Songs of Chandidās: The Rebel Poet-Priest of Bengal.* Grove Press, 1967.

Chakravarti, A. *Tirukkural.* Diocesan Press, Madras, 1953.

Dimock, Edward C. and Levertov, Denise. *In Praise of Krishna: Songs from the Bengali.* Doubleday, 1967.

116

Hart, George L. *The Poems of Ancient Tamil: Their Milieu and Their Sanskrit Counterparts.* University of California Press, 1975.

Ingalls, Daniel H.H. *Anthology of Sanskrit Court Poetry: "Vidyākara's Subhāṣitaratnakoṣa."* Harvard Oriental Series No. 44. Harvard University Press, 1965 (an indispensable work of scholarship and translation).

Merwin, W.S. and Masson, J. Moussaieff. *Sanskrit Love Poetry.* Columbia University Press, 1977.

Miller, Barbara Stoler. *The Hermit and the Love-thief: Sanskrit Poems of Bartṛhari and Bilhaṇa.* Columbia University Press, 1978. (The Bilhaṇa poems in particular are luscious erotic verses beautifully rendered.)

———. *Love Song of the Dark Lord: Jayadeva's "Gītagovinda."* Columbia University Press, 1977.

Nathan, Leonard. *The Transport of Love: The Meghaduta of Kālidāsa.* University of California Press, 1976.

Nayagam, Thani. *Landscape and Poetry in Ancient Tamil.* Asia Publishing House, 1968.

Ramanujan, A.K. *The Interior Landscape: Love Poems from a Classical Tamil Anthology.* Indiana University Press, 1975 (exquisite poems translated into English with consummate grace).

The Artists

Jaroslav Bech was born in 1957 in the Czech Republic and has lived in Germany since 1969. He is a psychotherapist working in private practice.

Richard Denner, poet and graphic artist, is a Vajrayana Buddhist monk. He lives with his elderly mother near Sebastopol, California, and is the impresario of dPress chapbooks. His *Collected Poems: 1961-2000* was published by Comrades Press. You are invited to visit his website: http://www.dpress.net.

Thomas Henrickson received a B.F.A. from New York's Pratt Institute and then moved to San Francisco where he exhibited his figurative paintings and sculptures. In 1968 he immigrated to Canada where he began creating visual projects using photographic media. He and his wife Martha, a photographic artist, live on Georgian Bay, Ontario.

Mary Kowit studied psychology and art at the University of Minnesota. She has been involved in bead-making, silvercraft, enameling, lampworking and printmaking. She works in information technology at the University of San Diego and is a freelance editor. She is married to the poet Steve Kowit.

Peter Najarian has written three novels and a collection of short works: *Voyages; Wash Me On Home, Mama; Daughters Of Memory;* and *The Great American Loneliness.* He has illustrated both the texts and the covers of his two most recent books. His nudes have been exhibited at The Artist's Union in Yerevan, Armenia, and his landscapes have been exhibited at the Hearst Gallery of St. Mary's College of California. He lives in Berkeley, California.

Vallo Riberto grew up in Illinois and spent 23 years in New York. He has been living and teaching in San Diego for the past ten years. His prints and paintings have been exhibited in New York and Los Angeles.

Peter F. Van Peenen studied sculpture at Princeton University and in Paris. He has worked in a variety of media, including ceramics, but his primary interest in recent years has been screenprinting, using facilities at Pima Community College in Tucson.

Perry Vasquez was born in Los Angeles in 1959 and has lived in San Diego since 1987. His *Keep on Crossin Project* was recently acquired by the Museum of Contemporary Art San Diego for their permanent collection. He continues to paint, teach and write about art. His various web projects include apollo13art.com, keeponcrossin.com and perryvasquez.com.

Jeanne Willoughby was born in Kalamazoo, Michigan, in 1951, graduated from Michigan State University, and received a Masters in educational technology from San Diego State University. She works as a Senior Training Specialist for Qualcomm and is both a poet and visual artist. Her illustrations have most recently appeared in the children's books *Do You Know Me* and *We Are All Peas in a Pod*, written by C.J. Minster. She collaborated with Steve Kowit on his book *Everything is Okay* in 1990.

Jorge Zarate was born in 1986 in Oaxaca, Mexico, and is currently a graphic design student at Southwestern College. He lives with his beloved family in San Diego. Previous works include t-shirt and banner design as well as freelance portraiture and painting.

STEVE KOWIT grew up in Brooklyn, New York, and after a stint in the US Army Reserves moved to the West Coast. When America's genocidal slaughter of the Vietnamese people began in earnest he sent the army a letter refusing to participate and spent the next few years in Mexico, Central and South America. After the war ended he settled in San Diego where he founded that area's first animal rights organization. He is the author of several collections of poetry including two earlier volumes inspired by the love poetry of India (poems that form part of the present book), as well as *Lurid Confessions, The Dumbbell Nebula,* and the well-known poetry teaching manual *In the Palm of Your Hand: The Poet's Portable Workshop.* The recipient of a National Endowment Fellowship in Poetry, two Pushcart Prizes, and several other awards, he teaches at Southwestern College and lives in the backcountry hills near the Tecate border with his beloved wife Mary and several animal companions. A former student of Zen, Vipassana, and the Gurdjieff work, he remains decidedly unenlightened.

120